Don't Cry

Mick Travis

Boys Don't Cry

ISBN: 9798644099924

Imprint: Independently published

First Published in 2020

Instagram: mickfntravis
Facebook: Mick Travis (@CityOfTravis)

Elliott P Reid

First Edition

Boys Don't Cry

An Introduction to:

Distressed Romanticism

Volume One

Selected works from:

2005 – 2020

Mick Travis

Instagram: mickfntravis

Facebook: Mick Travis (@CityOfTravis)

Dedications

To those who support & accompany my drinking, Shane, Mitch, Chris, Dan, James & Dec.

To those who offer their unconditional support, my Mother, Father, Bex, Niamh & Aisling.

To my beautiful fiancé Megan.

To the people who dare to dream like me, Dan Jepson, Mike Jordan & Andy Redfern.

To James & Will Hartland for putting a roof over my head for 18 months.

To my grandfather Pete, extended family & other grandparents.

To Wiggy for giving me a second home.

To Nan Dad.

To all the others: Stuart Smith, Laurence Cooper, Holly Parker, Ben Packwood, Simon Barrett, Sue, Tony & Mo.

Special thanks to: Megan, Chris, Dan, Ben, Niamh, Drew, Tegan & Aisling for proofreading.

Also to my Dad (Phil) for helping format & put this book together. Without my Dad, this little poetry book would never have left my laptop.

To all the Bar's, Clubs & Pubs that still let me in.

To all the people lost along the way.

"If you think I'm writing about you, I probably am." - MT

Contents:

Pete

The conservatories arm chair,
Once full, now bare,

His pictures still hang, on the wall,
His tobacco & pipe, lie on the side board,

Stories of how, things "use to be"
When manual labour, was done properly,

Forgotten faces, walk white care home halls,
But to tie a cravat, now that he can recall,

His nameless grandson, he confuses for a nurse,
His wife comes to check-in, they struggle to converse,

He's proudly wearing, a cheeky grin,
Until all the visitors, have come & been,

Behind closed doors, his daughter takes a seat,
They talk for hours, he struggles to eat,

His son in law, who he taught a trade,
Now a distant memory, lost in a decade,

His granddaughters, all so beautiful & fair,
So young & upbeat, with him, stories they share,

1

He's been brave & strong, but appears frail & weak,
Yet to our amazement, he won't accept defeat,

He's slowly getting worse, the whole family can see,
But his daughter still visits, even just to make tea,

Heart breaking words, he will so softly say,
"Can I go home yet?"
Mum replies,
"No Pop, not today."

(Dedicated to My Grandfather Pete Hearn)

Ode to Rum

"Rum, O' Rum, O' where could you be?"
The bar staff chime & carol with glee,

I've sought you, I see you, now can I taste?
Sweet like a first kiss, but with less of a haste,

Deceive me, mistreat me, but to my head be kind,
My time & actions mislaid, but love I now find,

You're my sister, mother & Fiancé in one,
Rum O' Rum, you're a curse on this son,

Rum O' Rum, my drowning liver wants home,
Rum's reply was to raise anchor, & sail to unknown,

You said you'd be kind, & take pity on me,
Your sugar cane fortress, I now want to flee,

Your black flag has waved, your bounty been won,
My emotions you've plundered, here ends your fun,

Rum O' Rum, say this ending isn't true,
I awake broken hearted,

Rum, I fucking hate you.

Two Dead Boys

Ladies and Gentlemen, Girls & Boys,
Let me tell you my account, of two dead boys;

My tale is dark, sombre, yet true,
But misery loved them both, & they loved her too.

One bleak hour, on the edge of night,
Two lonely boys awoke to fight;

Back to back they confessed their love,
For lady misery & the darkness above,

I heard the pleas and went to stare,
"Prepare for love's war", one boy declared,

Before first blood, one boy overdosed,
Whilst the other hung himself, from a near lamp post,

Misery cut the boy down & revived the other,
As he fell to the floor, he struck his brother,

One lay dying, drawing his final few breaths,
But before he passed, he cuffed his friend, on the head,

He crashed through a wall, making a raucous sound,
Into a creek full of his tears, and slowly drowned,

A long black hearse came to cart both away,
But the river stole one boy & there he floats to this day,

I watched from the side-lines of depression's battle ground,
The only eyewitness to love & loss found;

But if you doubt my story isn't true,
Just ask Lady Misery,

She loves you too.

Flattery in Silhouette

Decay is not obvious in shadow,
Or is pure beauty?
Be it the black shape itself,
Or it's cruel master,
Is it a mere projection of its captor?
Or a reflection of the soul,
Does it dance when you run?
Is it awake while you slumber?
Do we acknowledge it?
Do we consider it?
Can we hurt it?

Is it gone?

Her

I dreamt about you again last night.

Your flawless complexion,

Your shimmering brown hair,

Your deep hazel eyes,

Your warming smile,

Your soft lips kissed my forehead as I bowed,

I could feel your warmth,

I wanted to touch your inked skin,

I wanted to kneel before you,

I would change my life for you,

You fluttered your eyelashes & tilted your head as you faded away,

To leave me in the cold, dark premises of my room,

I can still see the freckles on your cheeks,

I can hear your soft voice whisper my name,

I can feel your body contour in moments of passion,

Then I sobered up.

No, It Isn't

Sweet serenity follows me,

Dance in my decadent lover's dream,

Sing me transcendent songs of your woes,

Grasp my hand where the two rivers flow,

Bated breaths under summers sun,

Orchestrate music to reminisce our youth,

Modes of transport take us to no particular place,

But I fondly remember our era, your smile & face.

Love on Standby

I'm a little red light,
Sometimes, you turn me green,
Push my buttons & touch me,
I wonder where you've been.
I wait all day,
Sometimes all night,
Engage me for hours,
Or minutes at a time,
Use me & abuse me,
Until you next flee,

In case you're wondering,
My love is a TV.

Train Wreck

I'm a train wreck,
Are you a Libra?
Missing! My Mind,
No Reward, Just curious,

She broke my first heart,
My second heart was anonymously donated to me,
I sent a postcard from the accident, but the stamp had blood on it,

Did it reach her? Has she got it?
Did she read it? Is she coming?

She's in her early 20's, & I'm late for something,
She said she's late, But it's early December,

Now it's back to school,
Now it's the end of me & you,

Missing! My heart,
No reward, last seen early winter,

I'm still a train wreck,
But you must be a cancer.

The Beginning of the End

Tears stream from blackened eyes,
As mouths await the taste,
Of the bitter sweet end,
How can love be so cruel?
Yet so controlled & seductive,
Please end this all,
Choked with a light angelic fragrance,
Nooses tied with thick locks of hair,

Poisoned minds with visions of shadows led bare,
A comatose kiss that stops worlds from rotating,
Cuts on skin from beautiful, yet pathetic sexual lies,
Taste the end,
Feel the end,
Hear the end,
Love shielded,
Trapped in a beautiful, hypnotic nightmare,

Leave it be,
Rotting in the cell of affection,
Starve on your hollow compliments,
Drown in a sea of sunken ships,
The same ships that ventured out to seek new love,
Only to realise home is where the heart is,
Or rather love is where you leave it,
And to let love die within you,

Lust Online

We met online,
She wanted to fuck,
I took her on a date,
She wanted to 'do it',

I bought her flowers,
She wanted to fornicate,
I bought her a drink,
She wanted to 'have relations',

I went to her place,
She wanted to 'have coitus',
I played Play Station,
She wanted to copulate,

I took her to my hometown,
She wanted to mate,
I went to her university house,
She wanted to get laid,

I wanted to stay the night,
She wanted to hook up,
I had a cigarette,
She wanted to get lucky,

I told her I thought I was falling for her,
She wanted to watch American Horror Story,
I wanted to fuck,
She wanted me to leave.

White Nikes

White Nikes,
Dim car lights,
Glowing Neon shapes,
Ambient bar escapes,

Your echoed voice,
My senses rejoiced,
You've got Chocolate,
I've got Vodka,

Renditions of being 17,
Dreams of being 21,
The reality of being nearly 30,
Whilst looking 24,

Bodies,
So many bodies,
Girls,
So many girls.

Three Sheets to the Wind

I've been focusing on trying to build relationships within the past couple of weeks/months, both romantic & platonic.

After its limited success, I'm now turning my attention to my neglected drinking problem.

I feel the results may be more promising.

I like my relationships on ice, & my Rum on the rocks.

Dancing Around the Subject

Love,
That's a conversation for,
Another time,
When I'm not so late,

Another place,
As this bar is crowded,
Another day,
Because it's not Friday,

Another week,
I've got targets to hit,
Another year,
I'm still in my 20's,

Another life,
This one doesn't fit right,
Another past,
Because mine doesn't feel like my own,

Another dream,
I'm a restless sleeper,
Another nightmare,
(See section about past.)

UN' I

Birth connects us,
Love embraced us,
Alcohol dilutes us,
Lust replaced us,
Time erased us,
Death haunts us,
Fear limits us,
Life breaks us.

From the Edge of the Deep Green Sea

On the tranquil seas inside my mind,
With oceans so vast,
Land you won't find,

Tsunami waves crashed my shores,
My City rendered baron,
Water rained at our doors,

Many a trinket swept away,
Mothers wept,
Fathers prayed,

The waves did stop,
The debris returned,
Love was lost, lessons were learned.

Enchantment under the Sea

Waltz away the pain,
Foxtrot around the sorrow,
Tango between the sin,
Quickstep with your lies,
Rumba to silence your heartache,
Jive with life,
Samba until you're exhausted,

Mambo until we talk again.

Music or the Misery

I feel that very few people,
Understand my plight,
But I take enormous comfort in,
Drinking all alone at night,

I also enjoy smoking,
But not the taste, or the smell,
To me these are comfort blankets,
To others they may be hell,

Like a small child might have a teddy,
I have Marlboro Gold's & Old J,
But I'm too old to sleep with a night light,
So don't take my comfort away,

You'll never feel truly lonely,
When you have vices & addictions,
Your depression might keep you company,
But my comforts are my afflictions.

Immobiles 4U

May your adversaries be,
Identical to mine,
Dressed in smart suits,
& easy to find,

They smile sweetly & discreetly,
In colossal board rooms,
But these enemies carry,
Their own inner gloom,

They wear Italian shirts,
But prefer a frown,
Lavish displays of wealth,
But always feel the clown,

Manipulation is key,
To take down this fool,
There mediocrity is clouded,
By using you as a tool,

Kill your enemies with a plan,
A handshake or a smile,
After this make them allies,
Or immobile.

An Encounter

Through the midst of being a creative 20 something,
I can't help but feel,
That loving you is more fiction,
Than fact,

That your undying affection is more of a rumour,
Unless the words have escaped from your own cracked lips,
I am inclined to not believe you,

Lie to me,
Deceive me,
You belong to the world,

But I'm here to watch,
Our civilisation burn,
We all carry several flints in preparation,
Held in our hearts & hands.

Golden Boy (Brian Jones)

"Born in a cross-fire hurricane" in 1942,
Lived a little boy,
called Lewis,
Who, the whole world knew,

Cheltenham born,
Brian Jones,
Formed & led,
The Rolling Stones,

On Bath Road,
He use to roam,
On Eldorado,
He'd call home,

The Grammar school,
At Dean Close,
By day he'd learn
At night, compose,

London called,
& he waved goodbye,
When he got on stage,
All the girls would cry,

He preformed at our Odeon,
& immortalised "Paint It Black",
He now plays with the "27 Club',
Cheltenham finally has him back,

He lives in the town with us,
You can sense him in the air,
Lewis Brian Hopkin Jones
(Thank You) for being there.

Drive (Z33)

This is it,
Just me & the road,
To a planned destination,
Or a journey to the unknown,

Confidence & independence,
Are the only things I need,
And maybe a little music,
Just to put my mind at ease,

I've waited so patiently,
& completed every park,
Just so I could pass the test,
& drive off into the dark,

My future is made more exciting,
Now that I'm out driving on my own
& with my new found independence,
I can mimic what I was shown,

I can't believe I passed first time,
With such patience & grace,
I made a few mistakes in the start,
But on the road I've earned my place,

I can't seem to believe,
I've reached life's next episode,
Now because of what I've learnt,
This is it, just me & the road.

Nottingham

I don't remember much,
Except exposed floor boards,
A standing bath, a bay window,
& your obvious flaws,

Your first year, your first house,
At least from what I recall,
I do remember the street name,
But not the number on the door,

I know where I use to park my car,
& dread the drive back at night,
I can still sometimes hear sirens,
& see the glow of the city alight,

We'd wander the streets,
& take Tram's to meet,
You'd go to Uni,
I'd lie-in & eat,

You told me once,
I've heard it before,
You said I'm "just a dreamer"
& nothing more.

Youth

What once, truly once,
But could not be retained,
Is now something new,
Where old can't remain,

People, places & faces,
All inevitable to change,
Like seasons & the weather,
But who burdens the blame,

Is it me, is it you?
Is it the both of us, if true?
Is it the emotions or the guilt?
Or memories of the thrill,

Did you purposely walk away?
Did you actively try and stay?
Did I try and make a change?
Was it the distance or the range?

Do I blame it on Cardiff?
Push the fault on Halloween?
Events might have been different,
Had your Uni sofa been clean,

Walk away into the grey,
Like a silhouette into the dark,
We'll forever remain strangers,
Remember the night at the park?

The Garden

Lost in Summer's hazy dream,
Gorgeous dewy grass,
Delicious clear streams,

The evening sky fills with Peach & Gold,
Ebony hair dances calm,
In the winds stronghold,

Gentle heat, bakes pale,
Innocent, blushed cheeks,
Shy flowers rejoice in Winter's defeat,

Sun kissed toes,
Connect with warm mother earth,
Sand eagerly awaiting, a waves next birth.

Falling For You In Florida

The heat comes in waves,
The emotions too,
A little black box,
With a big question for you,

Pat-downs & long stares,
Dollars, Quarters, conditioned air,
Water parks & swimming pools,
Had you noticed I'd fallen for you.

The Albion

At the edge of the world,
Shrouded in cloud,
Stands Tewkesbury's Albion,
Decrepit, yet proud,

Home to monsters, sinners,
A Poet & Twins,
"Your not from around here!",
"Only locals allowed in",

A place you can rest,
Your tired, weary heart,
Some hardly ever leave,
It's own decay almost art,

Fights use to be a plenty,
Robberies, only a few,
Nights are full to the rafters,
Always a profile you knew,

We carry no creed,
Accept every social class,
All races are welcome,
All genders are passed,

So in the dusky moonlight,

If you see our little pub,

Note, the Rum tastes like water,

& we don't serve any grub.

Ghosts & Other Night Fears

The floor boards above me,
Are dancing in the dark,
Not footsteps or shuffles,
But merry jumps in lark,

They creek & they moan,
Sing in a hush baritone,
Mysteries of their origin,
"It's the wind!", Megan groans,

But still I can't sleep,
My minds always in a race,
What would I possibly do,
If I saw a ghost face to face,

I think this house is moving,
I can feel it in my bones,
As if it had grown a pair of legs,
& learnt to walk on its own,

I hear a faint bell jingle,
It sounded like a metal wind chime,
I'm sure it was the cats in the kitchen,
What are they doing awake at this time?

Now I'm convinced above me,

There is a squatter or an unwanted guest,

The noises could be from a couple of bats,

Or an owl making a nice warm nest,

Now I've come to the conclusion,

As logical as my mind may be,

All these noises aren't animals or the wind,

But night fears that terrify me.

End of The Road

A little boy clutches, his mothers hand,
Prepared they walk, across the vast land,
With new shoes on, & crisp air in his lungs,
Eager to learn, but yet still so young,

As they venture forward, & age by day,
The boy gradually lets go, & off the path he strays,
Still in clear sight, under mothers watchful eye,
She's all to aware, of the day he'd say goodbye,

That day does come, sooner than she'd hoped,
She releases her grasp, & walks the undergrowth,
She's bestowed him wisdom, he's yet to discover,
But she knows one day, he'll return back to his mother,

The day soon arrives, just as she'd prayed,
He returns with a wife, & a child at play,
Now the mother is a grandmother, who carries a new load,
When they leave she waves, from the end of the road.

Wino Forever

So relentlessly twisted are we,
That sleep is life's minor luxury,
The quality of your tears, as judged by he,
Your inconsistent fears, on display to see,

Your seasons, they wither,
Like skin, on bone frames,
They bleed into each other,
Briefly staking a claim,

The last of evenings light,
Whisked away into the trees,
We heard them speak a language,
Then you let them be.

Ponderlust

Come as you are,
Take me as I'm found,
Read the lines on my palm,
Read them out-loud,

Take your time,
Stay on your course,
Promise me nothing,
The world is yours,

I've apologies to make,
For mistakes I have done,
Lost in a sea of people,
I love you mum,

My hero's are dead,
All my idols are old,
Young man, young body,
One tired old soul,

30 years wasted,
Or life just begun,
Should of saved some money,
Should of gone on the run,

Should of left this town,
With it's greys & its blues,
Could of got on a plane,
Just me, without you,

There was money to earn,
Bills to be paid,
Girls to be pulled,
Nights to stay awake,

30 years later,
Where am I now,
Sat in a bathroom weeping,
Making my mother proud.

Printed in Poland
by Amazon Fulfillment
Poland Sp. z o.o., Wrocław